ALL PILGRIM

ALL PILGRIM

Stephanie Ford

Four Way Books
Tribeca

Please direct all inquiries to:
Editorial Office
Four Way Books
POB 535, Village Station
New York, NY 10014
www.fourwaybooks.com

Library of Congress Cataloging-in-Publication Data

Ford, Stephanie, 1973-
[Poems. Selections]
All pilgrim / Stephanie Ford.
pages cm
ISBN 978-1-935536-59-8 (pbk. : alk. paper)
I. Title.
PS3606.O7465A6 2015

2015006037

This book is manufactured in the United States of America and printed on acid-free paper.

Four Way Books is a not-for-profit literary press. We are grateful for the assistance
we receive from individual donors, public arts agencies, and private foundations.

State of the Arts

NYSCA

This publication is made possible with public funds from the New York State Council on the Arts,
a state agency.

[clmp]

We are a proud member of the Community of Literary Magazines and Presses.

Distributed by University Press of New England
One Court Street, Lebanon, NH 03766

CONTENTS

1

SEEK OR SETTLE

When a desert dwelled inside of me,
I went there almost every day.
The first tree I believed in

let me gasp at its presence. The second
was a heaven of thin air and thorns.
The third tree just stood there. I heard its sermon:

Bloom. Shimmer. Touch something. Vanish.
In truth, I was nothing's congregant.
I followed what fed me, fell in love

with phenomena: cat's claw, bitterbush,
distance, thirst, the outreaching limbs
of every living thing. If I longed

to long for more than the next rain,
my desert taught me how to be less
than myself—a wealth

of evidence nobody read.
In truth, I was never pregnant
with reverence, except

for that time I drifted around
for hours, for years, getting
nowhere. Just here.

TROPHY

Our winter is no dress rehearsal. Is storm and stubbled hawkweed,
the dead deer in the meadow, a blizzard of timecard punch-outs
in the breakroom. In this season's cliffhanger

each of us is hunger's animal: the men in the mine,
you on the heart-and-lung, the mountain lion minding its kill
from under a neighbor's snowed-in porch.

The smokestack's white flag is the monument
we're made of, and as the urge to hit is often ours
when we hear the other whisper *hit me,*

we must have been the predator, too, waiting in the wings.
Remember the last ones, the blunt-nosed lizards
who taught us a constant tussling? We'll never know if they meant to kiss

or kill each other. As always, the lesson gets hazy. You come home stitched
and briefly tender, as any light, regardless of source,
renders us two ways and more.

THE PLACES

The places burn through us, so be bitterless.
Raise not your heart against the non-native species
nesting in the rain gutter. Your time will come
to hole up in the wrong house, a muddle
of fraudulent songs on your tongue.
The mockingbird perches and launches, perches and launches,

and somewhere is where you once, after last call,
found an elm or statue to be kissed against
heading into snow and sudden bareness,
pressed into a storm window that's still there,
off Route 6, under another weather.
As if this is who you are, the places stay in place

but you are only making coffee before work, here,
and here, getting the tossing of ashes all wrong, and here,
in the museum, planetarium, Cinerama Dome, recovery room,
the same play of light filling the screen:
everything you need to know, right here,
about extinction, quasars, sex
after surgery.

AWARDS SEASON

In the region of feeling
less than lost, antiphon
of gas-powered leaf blowers.
Cemetery, caution tape, carousel,
zoo. Last week's carnations
stay plastic and blue.
The prison bus bypasses
the semi's snapped axle
and I remember in pieces
how I made my way here:
it was sunny, it was Monday,
a few moments ago,
I opened the door, admitted
conditions: two fraying clouds, one giant
Kentucky Fried Chicken bucket,
scenes and streets missing
a murder to name them
after more than vacancy.

SARABANDE

Two by two we tempo the cloverleaf, swallow
blue downers with turn signals blinking
alone under Mercury, singing in stop and go.
In the room without warblers, room
full of sitcoms, few avenues lead us
to the edge of arrest, to a union
called mourning the luminous future
in photographs cut out and kept in our heads.
In the orientation, didn't you, too, picture
the glorious slime molds—*wolf's milk, tinder,*
carnival candy—doing their good work
while the manager tugged at his clerical collar?
We must be adrift in a really big church,
our silences taken for abundance
of worship, still trying to feel and feel
like a teen. To mean. Repeating: I meant
to be more and more delinquent.
To better the lacewing and treeswift
at temping. To do a sly kindness and do it
without sleeping. To-do: Sashay
past the guard gate, past Discount Liquors,
past the landfill's last wink. Be someone's favorite
form of protest. Invite all this infinity
to hammer me past sense. Knife
the guy-wire of evening and reel.

CATHEDRAL

Our sky is no less a special effect.
Someone slashes tomorrow's tires,
this month's billboard says *You could be next.*
Buildings fall, and stars, and dollars.

In the meeting for helping the children,
no one agrees on how to proceed.
Some of us eat re-heated pizza,
some of us miss the grasses we grazed in
as minor shirtless animals. Outside,

someone's ornamental plum
bursts into bloom like a shredded subpoena.
Two lovers break up on the public stair—
a voice that says *please*, a voice that says *no*,
a silence falling soft as gauze,
soft as a sugar pill dropped in the mind.

ALL I REMEMBER OF METEOROLOGY

(1)

For I did disintegrate, did break
on a slow day without gravity.
Before the wind uprooted the fig tree,
after the parade, between assassinations—
because it was xmas and I wanted
to survive, I let my words leave me
and tiptoed away, let the bright world briefly be.
I went to bits giddily, was all I saw
shattered, adrift without objects,
awake without eyes.

(2)

It was nearly a life
how I wanted to make light,
how day brought its anthems
and I drowned the day out,
left the news to the furniture
and bent to the whispers, to the tempests
I heard under actual statements, said no
to the sun's blatant pills and saints
as if an unseeing star could lease me
from time, could float me
to the previous earth behind words.

(3)

When I needed company,
I let windows fill me, and this storm
that ruined a tree while I watched.
It was a trilogy of weathers.
Termites, rusty nails, mouse incursions. Then
the theater of landing neither here nor there
when I could have been saved by a gift or a game,
by letting the blunt nouns invade.

(4)

When a cold wind proposes
rain for days, the mind confabulates
assorted bad endings
out of any available shift in pressure.
When every local god's gone global,
I find myself straining in evening's wake,
erased by passing skies and neighbors.
In the green room, New Year's Eve,
I breathed with the machine,
the machine breathed with me.
I was what I saw,
the gap, the interstice. In time
a marching band, the automatic cuff,
a voice saying *easy, easy.*

QUARRY

Breeze rifles the cordgrass
Streamlets tense their sumac ribs
Excavators enlarge our scars

One rebel in high-end combat boots
begs the ticket agent for an upgrade

The cricket modifies its song
(warm, hot, hotter, gone)

One clocked-in, profitless, coach-class I
thaws frozen chicken, scrubs the deep fryer,

buys imaginary islands
in exchange for real overtime.

OUR VICTIM

Ancestor of no one, claimless
and under all weathers, I elect myself heiress
of these green glints of bottle glass,
of the loose-knit zeros inscribing their shadows
across the expanding flats.

The unsung self takes seed in such badlands,
in a soil of shed wings and spent ammunition.
When night calls me in, I tether my silence
to stars and star lichens, entertain
the specimens of frontier dread—

field notes and ankle bones dredged
from a stream bed, our victim suspected
of living alone, of paying her debts
to the torched plateau,
of hearing the gun-range calliope keen
the ballad of *nobody's home.*

HAZARD MAP

In sunlight, at the door, you
had a story about your heart.
I had another about silence.

To make some progress,
we weathered each other,
became creatures and causeways
of the systems that kept us.

Me: *Like a murmur?*
You: *Like a trigger.*
And I: *Keep talking, keep talking.*

SETTLEMENT

Sweet capitol of misdemeanors, great skylit penitentiary
where appetites/credit/daylilies run riot

where windows and lunch breaks
are exit and sentence

I want to call a cold collision
and a blistering intersection

what weds these chop shops / squats / gun show posters
to our private insurrections on the downtown bus

where someone's dear felon has just been paroled
but not the extravagant yellow forsythia

and sirens invite us to notice the surplus
of tent towns ringing the diamond district

while only the sycamore obeys the storm warning
and all along the boarded-up boulevard

empties stray into brilliant assemblies.

TWO-POINT PERSPECTIVE

Five magenta and three pink balloons
snagged in freeway fencing, bobbing their brains out

and me, commute-faced, momentum-headed.
No one can see me dancing because I'm not—

that's the flame-tree stripped and stippled
and wearing its goddess wreath, waving sirens

set to Torture with capsizing voices
raised in self-defense. So singing, I forgot

to play to win. I laughed without cause, knew
all birds by their wingbeats. As if in a vision,

I saw my last paycheck in small dulcet fires,
and five bright appetites lapping, lapping.

POLITICAL THRILLER

In this scene, set
in the gorgeous grisaille of
what looks like Berlin,
the nicked-cheekbone hero risks
his new raincoat.
We want the odorless intrigue
of those cool Le Corbusiers. We do!
We, too, live in a city. In this scene,
the electric cross projects its red
against the hill where we bury our dead.
In this scene, our neighbor performs
for a camera, so labored
her bliss looks excruciate.
Meanwhile, on screen,
the district attorney's briefcase clicks open
and here come the killers,
swift and strobe-lit. I'm the extra
pretending to take cover
as the logic scatters like buckshot.
By contract, I cannot open my mouth
against the fake-evil greed
of the invented multinational
or pitch this other plot
in which a girl's mother's mother
sits in the kitchen, rests
her bad back,
tunes out the news.

INTERIOR WITH INSTRUMENTS

We joysticks, ringtones, barometric coronets—
choristers trilling in leaden vests—

let's train our tongues to name and invade
what hammers, pings, and plucks us,

to see and speak of mere appearance
as rainwater inks the alder's wrists,

lusters the downspout's tin acoustics,
diverts us from our ruin. As in:

all night while the ceiling leaks,
my rented house falls soundlessly down

in hole-shaped drifts and strands of pith,
and after I harvest the martyrs' wings

I'd bring them to my lips
if I knew how to savor an empty gesture,

the taste of peril given form and heft.

STONEFRUIT

Sweet groom, gravity is a weird glue.
It goes, as we do, from grievance to grave,
and the more I rehearse my loneliness,
the better I mimic your heart scar's armor.
Some of us are more done for than others,

and yet I planted that grab bag of dud bulbs—
glottal iris, fisted tulip, hyacinth
blue as a crushed thumb.
You knew better. The outlook
was ozone, slag heaps, mantle shifts. Still,

the thirsting roots. Skins puckered and crimped
over starchy moons. Dear time bomb
I beg affection from: sometimes I wish
you'd just rob me at gunpoint, but see
how the heat clouds unspool at evening,
slink off in gauzy strips? In the distance

I hear a ticking and think,
couldn't a stunted crocus open
absent all things that want to reap it?
Couldn't you last through digging season?
Like chucking a dead grenade in the dark,
I cradled each tuber and buried it deep.

LEDGE

I am already in my future.
It is a surprise rush of doves,
a Donut Time, and fresh cement.
It is nice the way a hand wax
comes with free new-car scent
and fireproof ceiling foam
and a hummingbird singing
like a spilled jar of sequins. I hear it's delicious
to fill the Jacuzzi with a drought on
and I have no prom-night stretch-limo memories
to compare my invisible marriage to,

but something's definitely in the air.
A hint of particulate, the sky coolant-rinsed.
Somewhere, an aviary is on fire
but twist-offs and all-night drugstores
survive. Pepper spray and invisible fences
are ideas in the world. Here,
in my future, a clamor of searchlights
can shuck us from our first names
and into the ocean called aperture fever,
called wolfing the night all alone with your eyes.

EXCHANGE

We feel these scalpels, know
half their motives—each frond raying
like fingers on skin,
like the grosgrain sighs of temporary workers
behind every Fashion Plaza.

Like zombies, the knives want us.
Unlike zombies, they want us
to arrange for the transplant,

to adopt the hardhat matter at hand—
one star's fire, cotton bleached
and combed for new money,
a choreography of seasons
to soothe the facts into song and dance.

Once, I lost that sentence's thread.
Once, I lapsed into uselessness.
I counted the smallest change,
registered every quiver
with far too fine a meter.

Now I try to exist between shifts,
mint my own currency, get better
by guesswork. In line at the bank,
plastic Christmas tree listing west,

under nine petite security cameras
swathed with wide red ribbons, I pretend
the disaster hasn't happened yet.

NOVELTY

Here's how I discovered
the next habitable planet.
I found myself again in transit,
barely advancing
behind a gleaming gold Escalade.
A giant, waving, fluorescent finger
pointed me toward a store called Aahs
(fake noses, unicorns, inflatable wives)
while the Queen of the Night
hit her high notes. In that instant, I saw
how every thing matters. Now,
as before, the sun sets behind me
while I iron tomorrow's work shirt.
Now, as before, I'm rarely at home.
What's new is, for instance,
this morning glory blooming
in the trash can from which it still
clambers—uprooted,
open-mouthed, trumpeting—
and how I get lost like it's nothing.

2

THE ARSONIST

The arsonist rouges the edge of the city
like suffering pranks up the edge of all things.

So we ready the car: bathrobes, coffee mugs,
the figments of our passing faces. We say

the cloud tower looks like Hiroshima
or a movie about Mount Vesuvius.

Over and over, our protests crescendo
to the acme of ornament: we write our goodbyes

in the hot tub water, heave our orisons,
fan the inferno. We only loved that lean-limbed tree

for the spark it struck in us, a moveable limelight.
If a dime's worth of cinder tapped us

on our smooth brows, how briefly we'd bear it.
Just take the damn picture.

SURVEY

Another wind OD'd on distance.
The day sat vacant. We lived
where the land never did meet the sky
and what we wanted was limit.
Asked the last candidate:
what governs this valley
where no thought stirs the chicory,
no enterprise axes
the lupine-bright gully? Answer:
paper cup, hubcap, soup can.
Facts and their funerals. As I grew,
I grew unequal to the mapping
and certain bright hoverers proposed
to pierce me. Tonight I drown
in moonlit thistle. Tomorrow,
faceup in the sun.

BIRTHRIGHT

And then the evergreen world
didn't need us to fall for it.

A cousin feeling, some kinship
in the nerve endings

named our pulse deciduous
and the furred and whorling woods

went missing. New cells thrummed
at the edge of development.

What tamped-down trail will miss us, then,
the mustardweed grown hip-high, viral,

while someone sights the sky in his rifle
and claims the whole skittish forest.

Neat heads bit red, pale bellies slung
skyward, a heap of harried flesh

on which deer season has lost its bearing.
Now no sundown catches us

blushing. No hound
comes hot at our throats.

AUSTERITY SONG

Let landscape instruct us
in the bitch-slap of sequence:
wet green fields, the Kum & Go's plastic thatch,

the hard-to-open seal on every remedy.
As the percolator snaps on,
as frost snaps the seedling,

we learn to parse the world
with the butter knife of acquiescence,
toothless, mute, equivocal—

We Poor But We Have Fun.
A tap of ash half-misses the tray,
pre-recorded chimes break in a Sunday.

And if, under pressure of large questions—
when to foreclose, how to untie a ribbon
after the body is found—

you still see one thing
without blinking—honey locusts
dappling a stockyard,

a procession of corroding silos,
even this stream of Pizza Hut fry grease—
you may do some reckless good

as, after a spell of rain,
dogwood and redbud ignite
streets named like a drinking game,

Broad, High, Park, and Main,
with such a largesse of questions—
the unfixed natures of grace, weather,

and the price of soybeans—
each requiring our subtlest measure,
and as on any moonless night

the universe offers us darkness enough
to know the mind's limit
and enough light to weave our way home.

PORTRAIT WITH FIGURES MOSTLY MISSING

Not a lick of this belongs to us.

Where the bramble cuts, gasp
of a needle's last lifting.

Fungal Haggadahs, yuletide wreaths,
five long-playing versions of Schubert's *Lieder*.
The phrase "seckel pear" on no one's tongue

as paintballers thrash through alder.
The chainsaw's fractious whine returns
as a fleet of Big Wheels jackknifed in driveways

and here—or maybe there—is where
our loose inheritance lost us—

a swan's razored beak, the ice-bound cows,
rooms converting mass to shadow.

ANNIVERSARY

Under a sky so wide.
Its two blind eyes.

Almost everywhere
we stray, no monument

to cast a shadow. Where saxifrage
roots its sweet rosette

in a hunk of granite,
that only a native lark or aster

should roam this deep
in grasshopper weather

is not what I wanted to know
in my bones. Found

among primrose and prickly pear:
the many ways she disappeared

and how the mind fidgets
through funerals. No snake

in the garden, no lizard wit:
between dinner and dessert,

little gods go berserk. Under steeples,
under neon, under gawking poplars,

wind whisks the lampposts
free of faces, collects

our roadside emergency kits.
Whatever I write next won't kill me

or will it? Whatever
sincerity is, it isn't pretty

in a mind that keeps on
composing its poem

when she could be alive
and singing it.

THE OTHER AIRMAN

The moon doesn't snuff itself out.
Does hover, tethered, over fallout shelters.
Tasseled rows of feed corn feel it
as do boys who, in dreams,
take tea with the enemy,
make love to the bombardier,
radio an aria in dashes and dots
over the sea's flaying mirror.
Did you find, Uncle, in servitude
the mind is composed
as a brain slice under plate glass?
The payload opens its petticoats,
eats a city, goes rococo
while a peony drops its incendiary head
and a child dunks her dolls in the pool,
clacks their plastic bodies together,
calls you saved, and who will tell her.

3

ADDRESS

Landlord, I am all pilgrim
lost in privet hedge and primrose,
caught in every kind of bind.

If you are so near and mine to please,
we must be neighbors.
Won't you grant me a gate pass
that we may gin the juniper, share a porch swing,
and drink to the ankle monitor of a day off?

I, too, like to watch the pageant advance
all evening between shows.
Weekends, I have tried to master
each of your tricky species:
larkspur, foxglove, black-eyed Susan,
the vivid cardinal at the feeder
testing the domestic kitty. But, sir—

what prophet in your salamander, so thrifty
it nibbles its own sloughed skin,
and what compass in a wilderness
so whole it owns and inhabits us both.

BIRTH STORY

Tried to conceive
the anonymous new,

spent half an island,
met a die-off of jellyfish,

wondered to whom we should sacrifice
our terrible breakfast.

Re: this and every emptiness,
the complete and authoritative ocean

swelled and thinned like a party trick.
Tide pools invited a casino kind of panic

and someone else's offspring delivered us
from inlets tight-mouthed as puritans.

GUIDED TOUR

What jerry-rigged thing
are they getting at, the pale-faced saints—
such a disco of hellos, or
are their flimsy hands just pointing, open,
to the giant pulley system
of the universe? Art loves the body's bulk,
glamours the body's bony luggage,
blings the soul with spokes and orbs.
Note the Gothic painter's genius
for granting figures fleshly weight.
Watch the unknown window-washer
blade the glass of touch and trace.

GULF

I spend my breath on words like worth,
keep the key to a home about to be bulldozed

when a really free agent attends the concertos
of yellow rudbeckia, notch-tipped, wind-sown.

If the lamina of man
are of vessels for water—

hydria, holy font, polyethylene—
where does our listening amber in?

Say the tongue's sudden sabbatical
lends us six white gulls. Say

six white gulls don't speak of lift
or any other easement

until a stainless pink electric disk
torches the sea free of sea lore. Then

let me learn to wear my going,
my one bespoke garment, just as lightly:

once a grain in Wyoming Province,
now a new vowel in the rift of my mouth.

OUR RAPTURE HAPPENS HERE

Not from, but deeper into

The bent-necked grass, the overpass

Fossils fuel our movement

A stand of aspen waiting for glaciers
A band of seers marooned
in their big myth

Workers stripe the mall lot
into car-sized parcels, and all of us drive
like we're country-sized

If my mind goes from prairie to meadow to pasture

If our industry earns no parcel of blue

If no rain, if missile, if lark call, if laser

Though the local hero roots for erosion
her homework consists of equations for staying

Her ancestor built that one-room lean-to,
maybe knelt and panned this bed

My gem, my germ,
spent piece of the species, let's

vanish and live a western end

EXPERIENCE IS A THIEF'S BEST FRIEND

To be that listening, sleepless,
always-ringing understudy

acting on small wavelengths, alighting
on this shattered windshield, that enormous

self-storage facility, how a record
pollution at coyote hour

debauches our dimming. Otherwise,
the deadbolt feeling: without,

scavengers drain Nyquil bottles;
within, behind hollow-core doors,

figures ink figures
in ballpoint blue,

shrug off what hand
taints the lake with moon

and lifts the water's fallen face,
sets the hill aquiver with penlights

plotting scores or orbits. Let in,
darkness springs each urge and limb

from day's instrumental grip.
Each minute hastens

our softest mergers: sky into body,
body into earth. Shadows

make progress, summon the mammal
now less employee, more loafer and lingerer

as a spider spins its agate sac,
as ivy breaches the brickwork.

COLLIDER

In hints and whispers
we augur our birth,

detect and plot the invisible,
burn to stray and verbing bits

while doves I notice alight on wires,
face the briefly abundant West

where one faraway unobservable instant
can't eclipse this tipsy cypress,

these hot-pink drought-season oleanders
bent on being a mystery.

I'd like to enter into evidence
the way the heron at hand arrests me,

how a more-than-hypothetical crow
dead-drops from slapdash scaffolds

to scavenge the meal we left
mid-sentence. It's like my eyes mean

to tell me something, if I could hear it,
inside the magnolia's supernova, or

within these collisions I call constant.

FOURTH WALL

It's the hottest day on record
again. Transformers spark.
A temblor rearranges the foothills.
I chip out my freezer in nothing but flip-flops.
Orb-weavers, bees, moths with pleated,
ashen wings—we're pushed to separate
lonely extremes. Outside my window,
a family of finches hops on the pavement
with beaks wrenched open in thirst
or tribute. I sit very still and feel too human.
One beat after the heat breaks, the hospital
discharges its high school track teams.
Sirens sign off, a dog keens its relief.
I go back to work and polish my act,
sing the first measure of any request
with an excess of what I'm not feeling.

YIELD

Glean from each globe
now gold now gone

a sweet decay. A dappled field
admits its faults

and is it so sweet? A fruit conceived
in ruinless green?

The untapped orchard
brims with hornets. Nectar's surplus
saps the urge. The drudge collects

its bonus, severance, sucker punch
and we're culled and flung,
sent home on furlough—
free to redesign our minds
around the open hours.

In the blink of the smoke alarm's
all-night eye,

no voice, no jingle, no digital ping—
just the glut of aftermath's
ache to be tasted.

AFTER I COME TO

I shred my fresh offers,
bail out the basement, fall
for the blue neon ribbon
on a strip mall. I'm alive
if I blink twice
at what might undo me:
moonlight on power lines,
the stricken nerve's singing,
a ground that will give
and give any minute,
how here's nowhere near
the extent of it.

TEMPORARY ASSETS OF THE VISIBLE WEST

Hello neighbor, window,
resplendent edge—

are we pollen
or investor

in homeless light,
in this ring-, ring-, ringing
of a solar conveyance,

of a deal double-struck,
now meadow, now mine

now staked and sickled
to mineral core as

pulsive the fund
risk seeds in the mind and

green the nerve
luck revels behind,
and as

to any switchgrass tract
comes a jackpot, fast-descendant,

cold with gridline,
flush of ask—so, now

is a matter of ore—or,
no—

the aspen moment that runs before,

swag and merch
of vetch and sedge.

CONTRACT

Magic video, travel time,
acrylic no-iron deadline sweat

the acropolis mood
our ruin makes new

though my absence accrues and counts
against me, I'm far too hungry

to fail to fall
for a sunset's burlesque,

each gold-lit leaf no loyalty oath,
neither declaration nor act of war

while styrofoam drifts the mercantile strip
and hot-wing delivery boys get high,

I find myself again at rest, subject
to dusk and the present tense

INFINITY POOL

Wherever awe is industry
and language surrenders its weather spectrum,

the ape of ecstasy Os its red mouth,
pixels turn on and pop one off.

At the reunion/interview/funeral,
the subatomic us
flirts with every other other.
The bride slips up and delivers her vows

to the statue garden, to the egret
reassembling its dream home
over riverbeds clogged with upstart palms,

to minotaurs turned marginalia
under the Under New Management banner.

IF EVERY POINT IS AN ORIGIN

in red nasturtium, atrium fern,
permanent eyebrows, kidney center

a humming waits and waits to be entered,
history rates us as hiccup, as blip,

as on a clear afternoon, flying a kite
from his office rooftop,
"not performing any work"

truant urge met skylight, bloomed

a tug, a lift
in the body's machine

a broke and booming business

ALMANAC

Thus comes the end of us.
Last rain. Slow file of the soldiered self
evangelizing the blacktop.
Where asphalt refuses its orchard roots,
brake fluid, tread burn, the world awash
in tailspin and windfall, in flimsy wicks
that won't stay lit. All over the *via lacrimosa*
where we so lately primped, cruised, juiced, and ate fro-yo,
where we loitered the plaza and nailed epic ollies,
a debris flow of cold calls, of winking red omens.
While the rain makes its pissed-off downpour sound—
swish-wish, swish-wish, swish-wish—
we pave our river over and name ourselves there
in felony orange over blowtorch blue,
each of us bearing a semiautomatic wince-grin,
a sprig of free needles for the good-news dove.

TO BRIDGE A BITTER DISTANCE

Yes, there is a here, here.
The sun favors it to a fault.
If you let the sand
sift from your fists
and build behind you
a silicate myth, you'll see:
before the smoke and ash,
before the punishment—

Here's the trick.
When the sun starts its blinding,
pivot. Lift your lids.
As collateral,
take your first impression
of the last tree you'll see
(for rooting, for the easy way
it takes to flame).
Then, surrender your name
to the pillar. It is a limit.
It is a bridge.

TRUE SURVIVAL STORY

To a boundless
aloft
I

do cross a trestle, fall
not for yonder
up and up

azure as

as error so wide
and so

to prospect,
pitch me down,

fit gift to hand,

hitch mind

to low and kind
economy—

grass, pinecone,
this,
our,

earthworm, please

any ballast,
grasp.

CURFEW

This is the body's return, a call to kill the fire—
leave the sky to its spinning and come in.
Do your days feel more like a strip-search
or a moon landing? A whiplash or a cake display?
Like good ballerinas, the stars keep their dying
well out of sight. We are, insofar as we are,
prepositional: in remission at the taco truck,
with an ex-lover, under a sonic boom.

Now we are tired from shooting our movie,
from tallying up the returns:
one flame-eyed adolescent
against the world.
Or: two red-tailed hawks at war
over one stunned mockingbird.
Now two mockingbirds dive-bomb a crow
who dreams a crow dream in which we don't figure.

This is the mind folding up its telescope
and opened to the rush and reed of the creek bed,
to gang signs thrown across a tossed-condom river.
How much of this concrete underpass
can I call home? How much exhaust
as the graffito of transport?
This is the world's wet tongue in my mouth,
its bridge and shadow and heron and crash.
This is the scofflaw mind's back talk:
I scrawl my initials on every corner—
even this gridlock conveys me.

ACKNOWLEDGMENTS

I am grateful to the editors and staff of the journals in which some of these poems first appeared:

Better: Culture & Lit, *Boston Review*, *Colorado Review*, *Columbia Poetry Review*, *Court Green*, *Denver Quarterly*, *Fence*, *Gulf Coast*, *H_NGM_N*, *Harvard Review*, *Hayden's Ferry Review*, *The Iowa Review*, *La Petite Zine*, *LIT*, *Lo-Ball*, *Oversound*, *Phoebe*, *Quarterly West*, *Red Mountain Review*, *Tin House*, *Typo*, and *Volt*.

My deepest thanks to Martha Rhodes, Ryan Murphy, and everyone at Four Way Books, and to those who made a difference along the way: my parents and brother, Nancy Bosch, Benjamin Weissman, Amy Gerstler, Darcie Dennigan, D. A. Powell, and Eileen Myles. Thanks, also, to Tala Madani. This book is for Charlie and Ezra.

Stephanie Ford studied art at Grinnell College and writing at the University of Michigan. Her poems have appeared in *Boston Review, Fence, Harvard Review, Tin House,* and many other journals. Originally from Boulder, Colorado, she now lives and works in Los Angeles.